EDGE BOOKS™

NATURE'S INVADERS

TINY INVADERS!
DEADLY MICROORGANISMS

BY JOYCE L. MARKOVICS

Consultant:
Dana A. Davis, PhD
Associate Professor, Department of Microbiology
University of Minnesota

CAPSTONE PRESS
a capstone imprint

Edge Books are published by Capstone Press,
1710 Roe Crest Drive, North Mankato, Minnesota 56003
www.capstonepub.com

Library of Congress Cataloging-in-Publication Data
Markovics, Joyce L.
Tiny invaders! : deadly microorganisms / by Joyce L. Markovics.
 p. cm.—(Edge books. Nature's invaders)
Summary: "Describes microscopic organisms that can cause illness and disease,
including bacteria, viruses, protozoa, and fungi"— Provided by publisher.
Audience: 008-012.
Audience: Grades 4 to 6.
Includes bibliographical references and index.
ISBN 978-1-4765-0142-0 (library binding)
ISBN 978-1-4765-3396-4 (ebook pdf)
1. Bacteria—Juvenile literature. 2. Viruses—Juvenile literature.
3. Microorganisms—Juvenile literature. I. Title.
QR74.8.M37 2014
579.165—dc23   2013004941

Editorial Credits
Aaron Sautter, editor; Ted Williams, designer; Eric Manske, production specialist

Photo Credits
Capstone Studio: Karon Dubke, 3 (hands), 28; CDC, cover (bottom both), 3 (top 4), 5
(inset), 15, 17 (both), 19 inset, 21 (inset), 23; Dreamstime: Ramunas Bruzas, 5; Getty
Images: EyeWire, 27; Newscom: Getty Images/AFP/Markus Scholz, 10; Science
Source, 14, Sinclair Stammers, 21; Shutterstock: Aaron Amat, 7 (hand), Alila Sao Mai,
9 (cell), Beneda Miroslav, 12, bezmaski, 25 (inset), Dariusz Majgier, 25, fusebulb,
10-11, Juan Gaertner, 1, Neokryuger, 7 (inset), Nixx Photography, cover (top), Oleg
Golovnev, 9 (inset), Richard A. McGuirk, 18-19, Zhabska Tetyana, 12 (inset); USDA, 11

Design Elements
Shutterstock: dcwcreations, foxie, happykanppy, JohnySima, jumpingsack, Michal
Ninger, sdecoret

Printed in the United States of America in Stevens Point, Wisconsin.
032013 007227WZF13

TABLE OF
CONTENTS

CHAPTER ONE
A DEADLY ENCOUNTER

It was a warm spring day in Georgia on May 1, 2012. Aimee Copeland was zip lining across the Little Tallapoosa River when the line suddenly snapped. Aimee plunged into the river below and cut her leg on some rocks. Aimee went to the hospital where doctors closed the wound and sent her home.

But Aimee soon felt sharp pains shooting through her leg. When the pain grew worse, Aimee went back to the hospital. There the doctors learned that deadly **bacteria** called *Aeromonas hydrophila* had invaded Aimee's leg.

Aimee was soon fighting for her life. As the germs grew quickly in her body, they made **toxins** that destroyed her flesh. Doctors had to act fast. They removed Aimee's foot, leg, hands, and part of her belly to stop the infection from spreading. Aimee survived the painful experience. But she will never forget her encounter with a deadly microorganism.

✖ bacteria—one-celled, microscopic living things that exist all around you and inside you; some bacteria cause disease

✖ toxin—a poisonous substance produced by a living thing

● Zip lining is a popular activity in scenic
locations like forests and jungles.

WHAT ARE MICROORGANISMS?

Take a close look at your hand. Would you believe that there are millions of tiny creatures living on your skin? You can't see them without a microscope, but microorganisms exist just about everywhere. They live all over your body and even inside of you. Some are smooth and round, while others are spiky like cactuses. Still others look like biting insects or wriggling worms.

The five main types of microorganisms are bacteria, viruses, protozoa, fungi, and algae. Many of these tiny organisms are useful. Some help people digest food. Others are used to make certain kinds of medicine. But a few can cause serious sickness. We call these nasty invaders germs, or **pathogens**. They are the source of painful diseases—and some can even kill us.

pathogen—something that causes disease, such as a virus, bacteria, or other microorganism

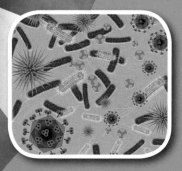

● Microorganisms come in a wide variety of shapes and sizes.

⚠️

WORST DISEASES IN HISTORY

Disease	Caused by	Date	Deaths*
Smallpox	Virus	1700s–1980	500 million
Spanish Flu	Virus	1918–1920	40 million
Bubonic Plague	Bacterium	1347–1352	25 million
Typhus	Bacterium	1618–1648	10 million
Tuberculosis	Bacterium	7000 BC–present	2 million/year
HIV/AIDS	Virus	1981–present	1.8 million/year
Malaria	Protozoan	2700 BC–present	1 million/year
Polio	Virus	1900–1960	200,000
Cholera	Bacterium	1800s–present	120,000/year
Yellow Fever	Virus	1400s–present	30,000/year

*Numbers based on worldwide totals.

CHAPTER TWO

BEWARE OF GERMS!

For thousands of years, people had no idea why they got sick. Ancient people often thought evil spirits caused diseases. But scientists finally discovered the truth in the 1800s. They learned that single-celled germs like bacteria and viruses are often responsible for nasty diseases.

BACTERIA BASICS

There are many kinds of bacteria. However, they all share some basic features. Each bacterium has a cell wall, jellylike material called cytoplasm, and a nucleoid. The nucleoid is like a control center. It tells each bacterium what to do and how to make others like itself. Some bacteria also have **flagella**.

Many types of bacteria help people stay healthy every day. But our bodies are constantly battling bad bacteria. These nasty critters can cause a variety of sicknesses. Some cause mild illness for a day or two. But others can cause long-lasting health problems or even death.

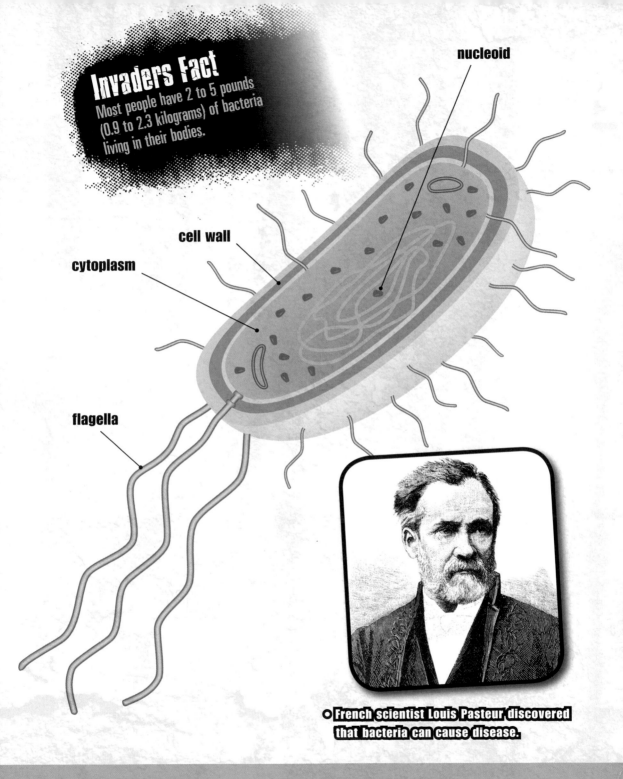

nucleoid

cell wall

cytoplasm

flagella

○ French scientist Louis Pasteur discovered that bacteria can cause disease.

✕ **flagella**—long, whiplike extensions on some cells that are used for movement

DANGEROUS BACTERIA

Many kinds of bacteria can be found in food. For example, different types are used to make yogurt, cheese, and bread. But sometimes bad bacteria can **contaminate** food and make people sick. In 2011 more than 2,000 people in Europe became sick with severe stomach cramps and diarrhea. Some people even died. Scientists soon learned that bacteria called *Escherichia coli*, or *E. coli*, was responsible.

● *E. coli* victims sometimes need to be treated in a hospital.

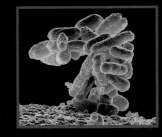

E. coli usually live in people's intestines without causing harm. But some types cause problems when people eat or drink contaminated food or water. The bacteria eat away the soft walls of people's intestines, causing pain and bloody diarrhea. These germs can also infect a person's blood. When this happens, the toxins that E. coli produce cause red blood cells to explode. A victim's kidneys may also begin to fail. If this happens, doctors can do little to help.

• **E. coli bacteria**

✗contaminate—to make something dirty or unfit for use

- The chickenpox virus causes itchy red blisters to form all over a person's body.

VIRUS REPLICATION

Virus injects DNA into body cell.

DNA instructs cell to make copies of virus.

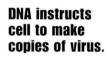

New viruses exit cell and find new cells to repeat process.

VICIOUS VIRUSES

Viruses are about a thousand times smaller than bacteria. Viruses inject **DNA** or RNA instructions into a person's cells. These instructions cause body cells to make copies of the virus. When the cells are packed with new viruses, they burst open. The new viruses then attack other body cells and start the process all over again. Before long, the virus has spread throughout the body.

COMMON VIRAL DISEASES

Viruses are responsible for several common diseases. Chickenpox, measles, and mumps are common childhood diseases caused by viruses. These diseases rarely cause serious problems for most healthy people. Symptoms include itchy rashes, red blisters all over a person's body, fevers, and swollen glands. People usually get **vaccinated** for these diseases when they are children. But those who do get sick usually recover in one to two weeks.

✖ **DNA**—the molecule that carries all of the instructions to make a living thing

✖ **vaccinate**—to give someone a shot of medicine that protects the person from disease

THE FLU

One of the deadliest viruses is also very common. It's called *influenza*, or simply "the flu." Flu symptoms include headaches, high fevers, and body aches. Most healthy people recover from the flu. But some children, elderly people, or sick people have weaker **immune systems**. Their bodies are less able to fight the flu virus. Each year up to 500,000 people around the world die from this disease.

There are many types of flu virus. Each year scientists try to guess which types will cause the most illnesses. They then create a vaccine to help protect people. Doctors recommend that people get a flu shot every year to avoid getting sick.

The Spanish flu killed millions of people during a worldwide outbreak in 1918.

● *Ebola* virus

⚠️

A REAL-LIFE NIGHTMARE

First patients become restless and soaked with sweat. A high fever and a throbbing headache come next. Spots of blood soon appear on the victims' skin. Blood also trickles from their eyes, ears, and nose. It sounds like a nightmare, but it's not. These people have *Ebola hemorrhagic fever*, or simply *Ebola*.

The *Ebola* virus is rare. It only exists in certain parts of Africa. *Ebola* is spread when people come in contact with infected animals or people. Health care workers working with *Ebola* patients need to be extremely careful. To protect themselves they wear rubber gloves, masks, and goggles. Unfortunately, there is no known cure for this disease. *Ebola* kills up to 90 percent of infected people.

immune system—the part of the body that protects against germs and diseases

CHAPTER THREE

PROTOZOA AND PARASITES

Protozoa are common single-celled organisms. They usually live in water or moist places. A few are large enough to see, but most are microscopic. Protozoa often look like insects or worms. Others look like plants or simple blobs. Protozoa are usually harmless, but not always. Some can be deadly.

AFRICAN SLEEPING SICKNESS

A tsetse fly is hungry for a meal of blood. When it bites someone, it passes wormlike protozoa called *Trypanosoma brucei* to the victim. This microscopic invader is known to cause African sleeping sickness.

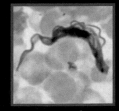

● *Trypanosoma brucei* look like wriggling worms.

African sleeping sickness is a rare disease that only occurs in parts of southern Africa. If left untreated, victims die from the disease. First they feel like they have the flu. Symptoms include headaches, fevers, and body aches. But soon the protozoa attack victims' kidneys, heart, and other organs. Then the invader attacks victims' brains. When this happens, victims often go insane. They lose control of themselves and sometimes attack people around them. Finally, they fall into a deep sleep and die.

Dangerous microorganisms like amoebas often live in warm, wet locations.

AMOEBA ATTACK

Tiny killers live in many warm lakes and ponds. Luckily, becoming infected by them is rare. They are **amoebas** called *Naegleria fowleri*. These protozoan killers often enter a swimmer's body through the nose. They then move to the victim's brain, where they start to feed and multiply. The amoebas eventually cause enough brain damage to kill the victim. Even with medical treatment, this deadly microorganism still kills 95 percent of its victims.

✖ **amoeba**—a microscopic single-celled organism that lives in a wet environment

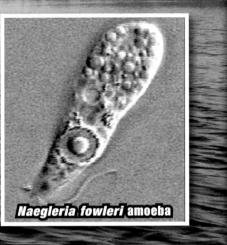

Naegleria fowleri amoeba

One of these tiny killers invaded 16-year-old Courtney Nash's body in 2011. Shortly after swimming in the St. Johns River in Florida, Courtney started getting sick. She began vomiting, had a throbbing headache, and had a very high fever. As she grew sicker, Courtney became confused and her eyes began to roll back in her head. Courtney's mother took her to the hospital, where doctors found that amoebas had attacked Courtney's brain. Unfortunately, it was already too late to help. Courtney's brain was too badly damaged and she died soon after.

PARASITES

Just like protozoa and amoebas, tiny **parasites** can cause people serious harm. Some parasites, such as ticks or fleas, live on the body of a person or animal. They latch on to feed on blood or dead skin. Others, like dog roundworms, invade the body to feed and multiply.

Many dogs carry roundworms inside their intestines. The dogs are usually not harmed by these parasites. However, the worms lay thousands of eggs inside the dogs. The eggs then come out in the dogs' waste. People can be infected by roundworms if the eggs somehow enter their mouths. Young children are at greater risk for roundworm infection. They can become infected when they touch contaminated objects and then put their fingers in their mouths.

Once inside a person's body, the roundworm eggs hatch. The baby worms then travel through the body in the person's blood. Victims often suffer from coughing, shortness of breath, stomach pains, vomiting, and diarrhea. Sometimes the worms can even infect a victim's eyes, causing blindness.

parasite—an animal or plant that lives on or inside another animal or plant and causes harm

DOG ROUNDWORM (TOXOCARA CANIS)

- ☐ found in dog waste
- ☐ can cause severe eye infections
- ☐ can result in blindness and death in rare cases

CHAPTER FOUR
FOUL FUNGI

No matter where you look, there is likely a **fungus** nearby. There are about 100,000 known types of fungi. A fungus starts out as a microscopic spore that takes root in a warm, moist place. The spore then begins growing long, threadlike cells. These cells keep growing to form various mushrooms or molds. Some fungi can be used to make wine, cheese, or medicines like penicillin. But some types can be a deadly problem.

DANGEROUS SPORES

People with unhealthy lungs need to avoid the *Aspergillus* fungus. It is often found growing in piles of dead leaves or in stored grain. If someone breathes in *Aspergillus* spores, a "fungus ball" may begin growing in the person's lungs. Victims have problems breathing and begin to cough up blood. If the symptoms become serious, doctors need to operate to remove the fungus ball.

• *Aspergillus* fungus

fungus—a single-celled organism that lives by breaking down and absorbing the natural material it lives in

TOXIC BLACK MOLD

The fungus *stachybotrys chartarum* has been linked to serious health problems for many people. Spores can enter people's homes through air conditioning vents or open windows. Once inside, the spores start growing as a dark-colored mold. The mold can quickly spread throughout the walls of a house. It is often called toxic black mold because it can release poisonous fumes into the air. These fumes can sometimes cause serious health problems like severe **asthma**, rashes, memory loss, and other brain damage. When black mold invades, people sometimes have to completely rebuild their homes to get rid of it.

✱ **asthma**—a condition that causes a person to wheeze and have difficulty breathing

TOXIC INVASION

Melinda Ballard and Ron Allison loved their large 22-room home in Austin, Texas. But in 1999 they knew something was wrong when Ron and their son began coughing up blood. They soon discovered that toxic black mold had spread throughout their house. As a result, the family was forced to quickly leave their home.

The house was torn down piece by piece. But the family already had serious health problems. Ron's memory was affected, and their son developed asthma. Their condition improved over time. But doctors said they can never be exposed to the mold again.

● Black mold can be a dangerous and expensive problem when it invades people's homes.

STACHYBOTRYS CHARTARUM

- ❏ grows in damp places like basements or bathroom walls
- ❏ can cause asthma and other breathing problems
- ❏ can result in memory loss in rare cases

CHAPTER FIVE
TAMING MICROORGANISMS

Billions of nasty microorganisms can be found almost everywhere. It might seem like there's no escape. But there are ways that people can fight back.

TREATMENTS

Doctors use medicines called antibiotics to treat bacterial infections. These drugs help kill bacteria. However, some germs have become resistant to these drugs. Doctors sometimes need to use combinations of more powerful medicine to fight these stubborn "superbugs."

Antibiotics don't work on viruses. But many drugs can help treat symptoms like fevers, runny noses, and sore muscles. These medicines won't kill the virus. But they can help people feel better until their bodies can defeat the invading germs.

● Doctors use many types of antibiotics to help fight bacterial infections.

● Washing your hands with soap and hot water is one of the best ways to avoid spreading germs.

STOP THE SPREAD

One of the most important things you can do to prevent infections is to wash your hands often. Putting your germ-covered hands near your nose and mouth is an invitation for microorganisms to invade. But washing your hands can kill the germs and keep them from spreading.

You should also be sure to cover your mouth and nose when you sneeze or cough. Every time you sneeze, you can launch more than 100,000 germs into the air! Simply covering your mouth can help stop the spread of disease.

People can also get sick from eating food that's not fresh or fully cooked. Harmful bacteria thrive in food that is not refrigerated. To avoid getting sick, closely inspect your food before eating it. If it looks moldy or smells rotten, it's time to throw it out. Also be sure to always keep uncooked meat separate from other foods in your refrigerator.

What else can you do to prevent illnesses? Stay healthy. Eat a healthy diet, exercise, and be sure to get enough sleep. Living a healthy lifestyle will help your body fight off the tiny invaders that threaten to make you sick.

Invaders Fact

How fast is your sneeze? Some experts think a sneeze can travel up to 100 miles (161 kilometers) per hour!

GLOSSARY

amoeba (uh-MEE-buh)—a microscopic single-celled organism that lives in a wet environment

asthma (AZ-muh)—a condition that causes a person to wheeze and have difficulty breathing

bacteria (bak-TEER-ee-uh)—one-celled, microscopic living things that exist all around you and inside you; some bacteria cause disease

contaminate (kuhn-TAM-uh-nayt)—to make something dirty or unfit for use

DNA (dee-en-AY)—the molecule that carries all of the instructions to make a living thing and keep it working

flagella (flah-JELL-uh)—long, whiplike extensions on some cells that are used for movement

fungus (FUHN-guhs)—a single-celled organism that lives by breaking down and absorbing the natural material it lives in

immune system (i-MYOON SISS-tuhm)—the part of the body that protects against germs and diseases

parasite (PAIR-uh-site)—an animal or plant that lives on or inside another animal or plant and causes harm

pathogen (PATH-oh-jen)—a microorganism that causes disease

toxin (TOK-sin)—a poisonous substance produced by a living thing

vaccinate (VAK-sin-nayt)—to give someone a shot of medicine that prevents disease

READ MORE

Owen, Ruth. *Gross Body Invaders.* Up Close and Gross: Microscopic Creatures. New York: Bearport Publishing, 2011.

Swanson, Jennifer. *Body Bugs: Invisible Creatures Lurking Inside You.* Tiny Creepy Creatures. North Mankato, Minn.: Capstone Press, 2012.

Weakland, Mark. *Gut Bugs, Dust Mites, and Other Microorganisms You Can't Live Without.* Nasty (but Useful!) Science. North Mankato, Minn.: Capstone Press, 2011.

INTERNET SITES

FactHound offers a safe, fun way to find Internet sites related to this book. All of the sites on FactHound have been researched by our staff.

Here's all you do:

Visit *www.facthound.com*

Type in this code: 9781476501420

 **Super-cool stuff!** Check out projects, games and lots more at **www.capstonekids.com**

INDEX

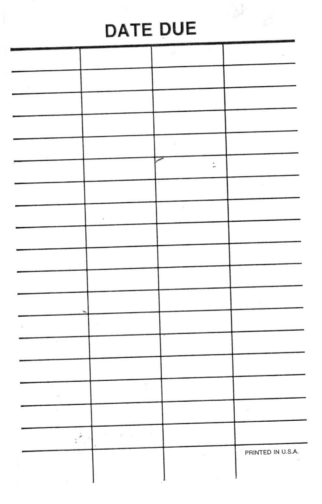

DATE DUE

PRINTED IN U.S.A.